Painting a Disappearing Canvas

Painting
a Disappearing
Canvas

poems by

Mark Saba

Grayson Books € West Hartford

Printed in the United States of America

Grayson Books
West Hartford, Connecticut
www.graysonbooks.com

Library of Congress Cataloging-in-Publication Data

Saba, Mark.
    Painting a disappearing canvas / Mark Saba.
    p. cm.
    Poems.
    ISBN 978-0-9838603-2-7

    I. Title.

PS3569.A15P35 2012   811'.54
                      QBI12-600140

Cover and Book Design by Mark Saba

Cover Painting:
"Tuscan Landscape One" (detail) by Mark Saba

for Joan

Please keep the world from floating away...

Table of Contents

Nicks of Time

A Humming Silence

Sons and Fathers

I am not trying to be journalistically witty, with this variation on famous titles such as Ivan Turgenev's *Fathers and Sons* and D. H. Lawrence's *Sons and Lovers* (or for that matter *I vecchi e i giovani* by Luigi Pirandello), but simply to suggest the autobiographical totalization that pervades this book of poems by Mark Saba, *Painting a Disappearing Canvas*. The actual title of his book is of course relevant, because this painterly image is not only a traditional metaphor for poetry in general, but is also connected to the author's experience: Mark Saba paints, beside writing poetry and fiction, and works as an illustrator and graphic designer. Yet the movement of psychological rooting and de-rooting is more deeply characteristic of this book than the aesthetic contemplation; so much so that I would have put these few remarks under the category *Life of a Man* if such a choice would not have been embarrassingly hyperbolic, beside encouraging false analogies: Saba's poetry is not specifically Ungarettian or hermeticist, and indeed is not particularly bound to the modernistic and contemporary Italian tradition in poetry.

Actually, with this fatherly-filial evocation I am trying to circumvent a label that I find increasingly inadequate: the label "Italian American," without the hyphen. The research and the debates on this theme go on, and they are certainly useful, but after about four decades of living in the United States (and taking some part in that research), I still am not sure of what an Italian American writer is. Mark Saba was born to a second generation Abruzzese-Sardinian father and Polish-Lithuanian mother, and he is an Anglophone writer; a writer moreover who meditates on the entanglement of his roots and who sounds as if he is tenderly worried that his children not be too bound up with this entanglement while at the same time he is concerned that they do not forget it. (Among the many poems in the book that reflect this meditation I would mention "Pre-Adolescent Sons", "Upon Rediscovering My Ancestors' Home in an Ancient Italian Town" and "Poem of Forgiveness" as particularly effective.) I am not sure in what sense or measure these elements, or any others in the book, make of Mark Saba an Italian American poet, and I find it more useful to briefly address the fruitful dialectic between the two national and complementary traditions (the Italian and the American) in poetry.

The roots of the residential or metropolitan Italian poet, who has a (relatively) stable collocation and linear story but at the same time consciously shares in the ancient and tormented history of Italy, reach so far back into the past that the sense of blood is weakened, and tends to become sublimated into myth or archaeology. But in the younger tradition of the "Americans"—the ancient and tormented genealogy remains the tragic privilege of the Native Americans—transplanted roots maintain a stark sense of blood. (Giuseppe Prezzolini's untranslated 1962 book, *I trapiantati* is still a worthy read.) As Saba writes: "I smell the past about me, / hanging in the trees, dug under / my garden. Body parts are / buried there. I see them / in my ancestors' eyes" ("Instinct"), and: "We've been told nothing about the bloodroots / of American trees" ("We've Been Told Nothing"). Of course every such generalization must be qualified; and, coming to think of it, Giuseppe Ungaretti—the "North African", "Parisian",

"Brazilian" and fiercely Italian Ungaretti–provides one of these qualifications. Still, this American difference helps explain the background of Saba's book, especially the aspect of it in which the noun *root* has to do in a certain measure with the basic physical experience designated by the verb *to root* in the sense of bodily digging into the ground, and also with the etymologically unrelated verb *to root* in the sense of lending support or encouragement. (I am thinking here of a familial sense of community.)

I hasten to add, however, that the dominant tone in this collection is not the darkly dramatic one exemplified above; neither is it a tone of post-modern complications and implications: there is no problematization here of the way the subject is present in the poem, no semi-auto-biographical distantiation, no experiment with hybridization and with post-generic writing. Furthermore, poems longer than one page are rare, and stylistic twists infrequent (although one may notice for instance the play on *life* versus *line* in "I Recall an Old Acquaintance Who Read My Palm" and in "Lines", or intense expressions like "my anti-self / wearing my father's gaze // long into his future, my past".) What we have here, then, is a collection of explicitly lyrical, self-contained poems where the vicissitudes of the poetical "I" essentially coincide with the biography of the author (although this coincidence or juxtaposition is not always smooth, as when for example a memory of adolescence is introduced by the critical title "Requiem for a False Life").

But, speaking of lyricism, I do not refer to anything emphatic or excessively self-conscious: the language of Saba's book is generally unobtrusive and down-to-earth–which, however, does not reflect any naiveté on the part of the author. Mark Saba is deeply read in English and American poetry (lines like "What one of us has done / will find us, one by one," in the quoted "Instinct", bring to mind a certain aphoristic musicality in W. H. Auden); and he knows how to metrically variate his free verse—as witness the traces of trochaic rhythm (in "A Pittsburgh Christmas"), and the constant use of enjambement, with its slowing-down effect on the poetic rhythm. In fact the above-mentioned entanglement of roots in Saba is literary as well as familial. For instance, when he opens his aforementioned "Poem of Forgiveness" with an image both elegiac and sinister: "I forgive you, Barbara Sobczak, my great-great-grandmother, / for smothering your twin infants at fifty-three years old, / heading from postpartum depression straight / into Alzheimer's etc.', one hears, beyond the family anti-romance, also a response, with a reverse perspective, to one of the minor masterpieces of American poetry: that *Spoon River Anthology* which, translated into Italian in the Forties, made of Edgar Lee Master an inspiring name for Italian poets. (The reverse perspective is of course the shift from the ancestral dead directly speaking in *Spoon River Anthology* to Saba speaking to them in texts like "Poem of Forgiveness.")

Saba's poems can also evoke, beside the vertical dimension of roots and genealogies, a horizontal dimension that may be called anthropological—and which sometimes appears as a dizzying sense of *spaesamento* when the American landscape, already Europeanized by so many place names, enfolds the guests (migrants? expatriates?) from the Old World: "Having left a party of Sardinians / in Lodi, New Jersey, I approach the GW Bridge / under studded lights, cars and 18-wheelers" (in "Driving Away from New York City"); or, more deeply, the problem of dialects and whole languages becoming undecipherable like the "jumble" of lines in one's hands ("I Recall an Old Acquaintance Who Read My Palm"), or flourishing on the edge of oblivion, as in this poetic duel of improvisation in Sardinia: " [...] There is only one chance // to get it right, a prehistoric rap / fighting to stay alive, even as their world disappears, / and all other languages // feign to conquer it" ("Last Words"). These lines, "intertwined" in the palms of the hands, or on the surfaces of different languages, or on the varying faces of landscapes, also evoke the plurilingual soundscape of America, where for instance the radio "lands on a particular song I like, / shifts to something I think is Greek, / interference from a hum of crisscrossing desires [...]", from the quoted "Driving Away etc.". (Descriptions like these always make me think of Vladimir Nabokov—one of the master narrators of the wavering movements of the expatriate, uncertain between fascination and rejection, through the American landscape.)

I indicated the unobtrusiveness of language and the lyrical chronicle of the quotidian as distinctive features of *Painting a Disappearing Canvas;* and indeed this is the general tone that lingers in, so to speak, the reader's ear after he or she has closed the book. "I Love Your Tears" and "A Poem for Joan" (coming one after the other in the collection) are some of the best examples of this tone: the former is a gently sensuous poem, and the latter is animated by the interestingly counterintuitive conceit that ardent love, rather than sending the lover on some flights of the imagination, is precisely what keeps him anchored ("Please keep the world from floating / away").

But the experience of poetry is radically unpredictable—and so it happens that, in my opinion, the strongest poems in this book are the few texts that do not conform to this tone of thoughtful, gentle exposition, but veer into a different space. In "A Garden of Refuse" the poet rejects the world of countryside or at least suburban bucolic serenity that seems to serve as background to most of these poems in favor of "[...] a moon-lit garden / of box springs and rusting cars, / a flattened pillow here and there etc.," and, he declares, "I'll laugh at the perfect / garden, curse it down, before those velvety petals // take me in, and Earth holds me silently / in the last laugh." (It becomes clear then, that the poem's title has a double meaning: "refuse" is used both as the collective designation of discarded, rejected, useless objects, where Italian would have recourse to the plural *rifiuti;* and in the sense of a decline of acceptance, where Italian would use the singular form—thus indicating a, presumably momentary, *rifiuto* of the graciousness, that can turn out to be constricting, of suburban life .) "The Immensity of Being" courageously declares its metaphysical ambition beginning with its title, as it follows the arc of a baseball "high above / a city-lot field, spinning its yin/yang / of white and white. The players look up; / they too are caught in slow motion, // uncertainty, complexity of being that entices / them all. Each has a new center of self— / thirty-five feet in mid-air, nothing / underneath, a changing perspective // of the immensity of themselves etc." A possible genealogy of this text is its response to the cool contemplativeness of Wallace Steven; but this matters less than the fact that the poem realizes the ambition of its title: it does indeed give us a glimpse of the immensity of being.

But the most challenging poem in the book is "Fire Burned Through the Sacred Heart of Jesus". The description of a burned house "marring the settled suburb perfection" leads to the description of one of the visions reported by Margaret Mary Alacoque (1647–1690)—a Visitandine nun, virgin and saint who was one of the early proselytizers of the devotion to the Sacred Heart of Jesus (or Sacred Heart for short)—and the text closes with what sounds like a direct quote from her. This is the only poem in the book that can properly be defined as mystic; not because of the described devotional background, but because of the wildness that bursts out of this background. Devotion and mysticism are not incompatible—in fact, there is a synergism between them—but they should not be confused: the devotional is edifying, whereas the mystical is deconstructive. It takes some courage, then, to address the mystic dimension, not only in poetry but in life generally. This is especially true in the mental landscape of contemporary American literature, where religious poetry, above all in its Christian aspect, is not particularly encouraged and, when given a voice, is usually reduced to a generic universalism or to defensive qualifications. In such a context, the devotional is usually regarded as mere folklore, and the mystical with at least diffidence; hence the significance of Saba's poetic statement.

Having dwelt, however, on the continuity between biography and poetry in this book, I hasten to add that I do not know anything about Mark Saba's religious convictions or lack of them (nor do I plan to ask), and that his writing does not fall into the trap of confessional poetry—a concept where the adjective contradicts the noun. In fact, Saba's poetic reflections on spiritual experience are refreshingly informal and welcoming toward doubt: in the poem "Doing Push-ups," the author says: "[...] I can do a hundred / or two, or sit down and read / till I'm blue in the face. // Will I ever have enough energy to say a prayer? [...]"; and in "Days of Love:" "Questioning religion, and whether I've measured up, / I'll go blindly. All will be lost to these / days of love [...]." The above-mentioned text about the Sacred Heart, then, can be

Great Expectations

I believed in the fall
that I could be in love,
that I could sit in a musty,

school-smelling room and think
until my heart ached out
and I was called to attention.

I believed that Pip would marry
Estella long before I read the end
while watching an autumn rain

throw yellowed leaves at the old school's
windows, and the marmish junior-high teacher
give her life to find one set

of wandering eyes. My love and I
exchanged glances; Miss Havisham looked down on us
from a chalk pastel sketch I'd made

and hung on the corner board. As the season deepened
I found occasion to press my lips deeply
into my beloved's, to gather her into

my adolescent arms, their strength
pure and inconclusive. I believed
there was no ending, only a dark autumn

sky, the spirit of a heart-broken woman
watching over us, and the open, ongoing
pages of me.

Just Before

Things were nice just before
all hell broke loose,

before my brain was reduced to hormones
and nuns left the convent

to think about what they had lost.
We sat in five straight rows of ten,
stood in line at the lavatory
and recess grounds, counted our pencils

and crayons' shades of blue.
There was nothing lacking but time,
for The War led to riots
and riots led to changes

in the way people saw themselves,
but we held on quietly
to the nunlike black and white,

believing in our colored constructions
as they covered the walls.

My Mother Straightens Her Babushka

And pulls its gossamer ends gently,
back and forth, as if rocking
a row boat under her chin.

She turns her head this way and that,
presses her lips to firm up lipstick,
leaves the mirror and its selfish ways

on her way to a dinner date, bowling game,
Mass. To me she is just another
pretty mother, but to others

she is a Polish-American beauty, unreleased
from three generations of flowery
babushkas, Anglo-Saxon words

in her head, a freshness on her brow
that cannot be covered. It's that paradox
that holds her mirror image

in me. Now she is old
and I am going gray,
our lives in the balance

of forward and back. In Poland
young women won't wear babushkas.
They want to look American,

as pretty as Britney Spears
and Cameron Diaz. And if they ever have children
none of them will find a mystery

in their mothers' lovely faces
as they stand before their dressing mirrors
and dish up beauty with a dash of past.

Polish Men

Kujawa, Kubiak, Radziukinas—
these Polish men and one Lithuanian.

Nowowiejski, Brodola, Domian—
One devotes his time to tropical fish.

Another a gym instructor; or uncle in the attic
who sleeps before a life-sized crucifix.

Gardeners, beer brewers (drinkers)
who hug you, kiss you in a capsule

of snuff, cigars, beard stubble, sweat—
who eat chocolate-covered bumblebees,

blood sausage, turtle soup; drink tomato juice
and buttermilk. They come all scrubbed,

shiny pink faces ready for the wedding,
baptism, funeral, communion party

before the tie comes off, the shirt loosens—
hairy arms and big, big smiles

teasing the women, fooling the children—
these Polish men, the butt of so many

bad jokes, shoring up my history;
leaving me no guilt, no expectations,

no explanation for their gleaming eyes.

On the Eve of the Anniversary
of My Father's Death

We used to go to church that day,
the four of us carting our bodies
up to Saint Albert's before school began,

the scent of summer on our lips,
the stirrings and new beginnings
free to roam about the empty pews.

At The Offering the priest would say
his name, and we would bow our heads
as if the church weren't bare.

I would note the open sanctuary door
where light pine panels led
to other doors, and then to outdoor light

as it filled the little room
with reflections of bordering trees,
their sweet dying blooms

coalescing with the white of candles,
light, and lore.

A Pittsburgh Christmas

In two days there may be snow
dark over the black waters of the Allegheny
and Monongahela. All night it will fall,

starting in upper layers of precolonial green,
down through the levels of coal furnace soot
and sulfuric steam, then ending in a flickering

that confuses even those who are asleep
in their ancestors' dreams. On waking they will not know
what age it is, or what fills the morning air.

Will it be candlelight commingling
from the boughs of Christmas trees?
Or the sweet breath of young lovers

kissing in the cold? One thing is certain:
There will never be clear days of nature's
pure intent. They will be soiled with ours,

and the snow will fall this side white,
that side gray; leaving wide spaces amid flakes,
a view we piece together, a time

we break away.

This Poem Is For

This poem is for Miss Kopycinski,
my second grade teacher, who bought
Edith Gronsky's First Communion dress

(whose mother had just died
leaving eight children).

This poem is for Guglielmo Marconi
who allowed me to hear "Where Did Our Love Go"
on the car radio while standing behind the front seat
as my mother drove past the Passionist convent
that same year.

This poem is for Mr. Fitzpatrick the art teacher
who stood every Saturday morning before five hundred kids
in the music hall of Carnegie Museum in Pittsburgh
and pulled magical rabbits from his easel.

This poem is for the girl I met in Italy
who sent me postcards after I'd returned
which I never answered.

And this poem is for Edith Gronsky
after she came back to school, her pale face
and wispy white hair even more
pale and wispy now—

And for the students who whispered to one another
back near the coat closet until Miss Kopycinski
hushed them back to their seats, her blemished complexion
blooming a soft pink.

This poem is for Miss Kopycinski,
for how she blooms in us.

A Natural History of Pittsburgh

There is love heaped on the dried grasses
swirled frozen at the end of the Bloomfield Bridge,

love lost among the staggered row homes,
laid in their brick and poured into front steps.

Love lies buried along the riverbeds
where blast furnaces burned; it rises

through wooded hills to hilltop communities,
settles, moves, and is moved again.

Only the will of nothing defies it,
that which allows no work, no change—

nothing in place of nothing—when all stops
but the trickle of rain tearing down

landscapes. When love blows through the winding hills
of Pittsburgh it comes to no rest, but pins

everything there in place, conducting voices
and the souls of working hands, as willfully

as the doldrums of indifference.

On the Day I Was Conceived

A streetcar rattled by my parents'
apartment; snow fell
in early March. A city slept

under its blanket of soot, and my mother
had a vision of her childhood.
On the day she was conceived

the first leaves fell from my grandmother's
favorite tree—a dogwood misplanted
by an errant bird—bordering her square

of dirt backyard. On the day *she* was conceived
my great-grandparents passionately
tossed in bed; a pillow fell

to the floor, and a new-world phantom
watched from an empty corner.
On the day my daughter was conceived

I forgot who I was; my wife fell asleep
and a car pulled stealthily
out of the common driveway.

We dreamed of other worlds:
of future nights in quiet homes
and stars that lead nowhere.

Requiem for a False Life

I am writing this while plans are underway
for my fifteen-year high school reunion
which I will not attend.

I am writing a cursory note
on the desk that once bore pen engravings,
pencil dust, and splotches of heavier ink
called paint.

For it was here I did
those oils, wrote notes to female friends,
or stared long into the grain
of weathered wood, until my father
stared back at me, and called me
to a secret life, called art.

Those late afternoons after school
or snowy Saturday evenings
found me forging a bridge
from circumstance to gentler eternity,
from ways I had taken in stride
to glimpses of another face,
another figure cutting silver
through the air. And now that boy

is on the other side.

Maria Antonia Waits for Her Twin

Someday, she said,
she would send her brother cookies
in America.

She would weave
the world's largest blanket
from scraps of clothing
and bed-lining
to hold the cookies in.

And so she sat from eighty
to eighty-nine, at first lucid
enough to remember thread lines,
then brittle as *biscotti*
she had lined up for years
above anyone's reach.

She would reach down for string
and tie knots around her knuckles,
gather enough cloth to hold her afloat
above the frightful ocean.

She would come saying, "It's almost done,"
even as they read the letter again
to her, and no tears welled,
but she kept on sewing.

Venus Is Closer Now

Venus is closer now
than I remember it.

She gleams more fiercely at me,
makes me note the difference
between planet and stars,

and now I realize that things
aren't what they used to be.

At sixteen I jogged to my grandmother's
three miles away, spent the afternoon
pulling weeds and cutting grass,

and called home on a dial phone
that put every one of us in place—
my mother, my grandmother, and me—

with every round number, every spin
of the cranky old wheel: a solar system
with me at the center.

Now there are no centers, only flights
from one view to another, a button to press
that brings us together, a woman

who slips down from the sky.

I Love Your Tears

I love your tears,
your arms folded close
to your body in the shadow

of early evening. I love that
confusion, the emptiness I know
that will do nothing but fill.

In your mouth, a rush of words
tumbles over a crooked lip.
I love that lip. I love that night

as we lie unsteadily together
and half-sleep, your tossing
keeping me from rest.

A Poem for Joan

Please keep the world from floating
away, the air from chilling my body,
the ground from shaking.

Take care not to pass by the market;
bring nothing with you today.

Let appointments fall by your feet;
keep only the unspoken.

Take this poem away from me.

Do not come intruding
into my life: become
my life.

Make me unaware of my body
unless I am with you.

Let our spirit reside
with or without bodies.

Let all histories bow down to ours:
the news of our planet cannot compare
to one life lived in another.

Sam

He left me for that wilderness
of heaven, the one nuns looked up
in the Baltimore Catechism, then

passed on to us Vatican Two kids
still tidied up from the fifties
but moving fast toward the edge of a precipice

where they too would fall. His image
came only from black-and-whites, all smile,
wavy dark hair and a hand-tinted face.

He and my mother became petrified
by that look, and all the Ozzie and Harriet
that went with it, as I stumbled along

in the uncertain light of the present.
But what if he'd had a different life?
One like his father's, maybe:

a Sardinian shepherd born of stargazers
and women who hummed
when they did the wash. Or how about a soldier

drunk on the streets of postwar Paris,
half-heartedly waiting for his ship
to the charted waters of a new, unchecked

America? I like the one of him
leaning forward at a crowded café table,
chain smoking, hair wild and unwashed,

a four-day stubble on his chin
and bright epiphany in his black eyes.
Then there is the day he walked down the street,

nothing in particular holding his attention,
yet everyone noticing his elegant body
as it called up all futures and pasts,

a flirt on his beautiful face as it made
strangers fall in love with him.
Yes, even if that meant

I would never be born.

Yes, I'm Still Here

(for my father)

Yes, I'm still here
waking up every morning with cloudy
eyes, waiting for the air to clear.

Yes, the mock orange still puts out stars
and downy woodpeckers cling to the sills.
I've struck up a painting or two, written novels

while my children slept. Yes, I'm going gray
a bit all over. So many views from my windows
obfuscate those early days of bumping into you.

The black and white Kennedy years left
for a color Zenith; for songs that, I'm sure,
would have made you cry. What else

would you like to know? Weather reports
are looking like those of your Depression childhood.
A couple of wars here and there. Not much else.

One thing worries me though: I've written this poem
before, mailed it off to the breathless sky.
But you, from your blank home, have not replied.

Last Words

My grandfather was born in Sardinia.
Nonnu meu este naschiddu
in sa Sardinna.

He spoke an uncommon language,
a local Latin that never went away
resting on Phoenician and Carthaginian song.

Two brothers and a twin sister
looked after him when their parents died,
then winds whistling through

the rocky hills of Bultei beckoned
him away. He landed
in the steel mills of Pittsburgh

coughing up coal dust
and marrying a woman
who thought he spoke her language.

But as he lay dying
she mistook key words of his
for others; he had lapsed

into his past, and now
she could not reach him.
In Sardinia two men will create a sung poem

on the spot, opening up worlds
that lie under the heart,
battles for expression

that must be won. The game
can be fierce: each man crooning
to outdo the other. There is only one chance

to get it right, a prehistoric rap
fighting to stay alive, even as their world disappears,
and all other languages

feign to conquer it.

I Recall an Old Acquaintance Who Read My Palm

I recall an old acquaintance who read my palm
at a costume party, and try to connect my life
with her remarks. This afternoon I study old pictures

to find my father's hands. I discover the long, relaxed fingers
that belong to the type "water," like mine.
Once, as a ten-year-old, they made me hold them out

before an audience of great uncles and aunts.
"He has his father's hands," my mother said.
(There was magic where I couldn't tell.)

My three-year-old has hands like mine.
"Let me read this," I say, taking one and opening
his palm. I study the lines, trying to remember

what the old friend said. But there is only a jumble
of things I cannot tell—repetitions of lines
growing from ancestors as unknown to us

as those to come. "What does it say?"
he asks. "I don't know," I offer.
But I know we must study our hands

to know our intertwined lives, work
that must be completed, and scars
of what we have wrought.

Days of Love

After the late rain, the cool sun,
the chill and elusive clarity of sky,
he fell asleep in mid-afternoon, when all our intentions

had left us, and the feeling that remained
was one of utter complacency, acceptance, a relishing
of what had been offered us. The weather cells outside

ceased their eternal rhythm, while I carried the quiet
with a book. There may never be days again like this:
accidental, unguided, a father relinquishing every responsibility

except to his croup-stricken son. The world would not have it so.
I felt my old deathbed on the other side of the moment—
Questioning religion, and whether I've measured up,

I'll go blindly. All will be lost to these
days of love; and nothing else will have made sense,
nor score, but a time that was known as pure.

Lines

Sunfish suspend themselves over deeper
cloudy water, making their lives
more or less visible.

                    My son and I
fish their pond for bigger things,
the grist of dreams: our lines
in and out of the water; swallowtails
making zigzags of summer air
above us. And all around the quiet thunder

of blooming laurel. He catches
the biggest fish of the day, but remains
intently calm, reeling in a mystery
that shows up half his size.

We both watch the line—its guided,
wandering force. A struggling fish
makes no sound under water, and we strike
at the right random moment.

Already, too much has been imprinted
on the backs of my son's eyes.
Where is the ghost of that invisible line?
How do I tell him his best friend is dying?

Dismembering the Swing Set

Some things only a father knows—
a construction of paradise
under the changeable sky,

a music only he hears
as his children dance, blinded
by youth-time, on the tended lawn.

Some things collapse
inaudibly, the heart of his intention
gone insignificant—and no one

notices that things have never been
as they are, nor as they will be,
but as they were. Birds cross over

such unintended worlds, drawing strings
that line the air to entangle ghosts
at twilight. Then the house

changes shades, the yard is
overgrown, and the father surrenders his chores
to the shadow of things to come:

a toddler's wary walk sure-footed,
the end of a perfect day.

Pre-Adolescent Sons

Boys grow long; limbs lighten
and faces grow narrow profiles.
One nearly spent summer day

they dream of teenage peers
spinning soccer balls, daring leaps
that confound imaginations.

Soon they get up and leave boy shadows
pressed into grass; they find another field
away from spectators and coaches

and make up their own rules.
One kicks past a defender's grip;
another dives to the ground only

for the sake of diving. We are still
lost in the older boys' game, intent
on willing its randomness.

But the eleven-year-olds, they've seen
enough. This may be their last summer
of remembering how everything was never

within reach: the far end of the field
and time it took to get there, half-hearted headers
and passes never made. In a year

they'll grow sheathes of muscle
around those hollow limbs.
Their fathers will watch with a new empathy

as another mold breaks, runs,
and soft cocoons lie fading on the grass.

Nicks of Time

Depression Women

You know the type: Eleanor
was one of them
in her baggy dresses—

big-bosomed, filament
hair pressed down,
wide legs atop no-nonsense

shoes. Caricatures
of themselves, these figures
blurred a landscape that never

gave them time. They were
all smiles, suffocation
for small children,

yards of fat from eating
while you can. Was your grandmother
one of them? Did she grimace

while separating the flour
to make a well for the eggs?
Did she not remember

the prettiness of her youth
when she fell for life
and then stayed centered

in its dusty core?

Upon Rediscovering My Ancestors' Home in an Ancient Italian Town

The seated *anziana*, ninety-one, peers off
into nothing. Whitewashed stone
blinds her blue eyes: four walls

surround the town's oldest, smallest
square. *Rabbits, chickens, goats,* she says,
two pigs and a cow. Families whose walls

made a rectangle. By night they tucked the animals
underground, closed the small arched doors
and waited for the roaming rooster's crow.

Ask her, says the nurse, she remembers everything.
My great-grandmother? Almerinda?
Rinda, we called her. Bella donna.

They lived there, down in front.
Another woman feeds cloistered chickens,
the only ones left. Tourists, still asleep,

make no noise in their rented rooms.
Now, she says, *più stranieri che paisani.*
More tourists than locals.

Her hand, still sure, swings a flowered shawl
up to her shoulder. Then the eyes return
to me: a ghost at dawn, *straniero*

who speaks the language
of three generations gone. I ask about
the strange little door I had once drawn

down at the gallery's entrance.
Covered up. And the big stones surrounding?
Renovated, after the quake.

A smile lights, then disappears. The nurse
takes another puff of cigarette.
The chicken feeder is gone.

Eh, Tutto finisce, she declares.
Everything must come to an end.

Poem of Forgiveness

I forgive you, Barbara Sobczak, my great-great-grandmother,
for smothering your twin infants at fifty-three years old,
heading from postpartum depression straight

into Alzheimer's, and no one to show you the way.
I forgive you, great-grandad Antanas, for having
fifteen kids and then checking out with the bottle.

I forgive you, Nonnu Saba, for not paying enough attention
to my grandmother, whom I loved. I forgive my uncle
for selling his artist's soul to commerce to raise

my brotherly cousin. I forgive my uncle's brother
for thinking he could save us in war—for now
I cannot speak to him. I forgive my mother's mother

for withdrawing into silence, then speaking only in religion.

I forgive my father for dying.
I forgive my mother for having to raise us
only as a woman.

And I forgive myself for heading down
the weedpath of words, to speak in a language
they will not understand, one

that may not be forgiven.

Driving Away from New York City

Having left a party of Sardinians
in Lodi, New Jersey, I approach the GW Bridge
under studded lights, cars and 18-wheelers
slowly congealing—lanes disappearing
without a trace.

We crawl, one by one, over the Hudson's
abyss, eyes fixed on a scintillating skyline,
determined to overtake it, but ending up
merely shifting specks. Piping adorns oily concrete
in horizontals. Signs lead to New England parkways,

the Whitestone, Bronx. My radio scans
traces of human voices: a pop hymn
in a language undetermined, rock anthem
thirty years old, DJ offering a prize
to a Riverside man too excited to talk.

It lands on a particular song I like,
shifts to something I think is Greek,
interference from a hum of crisscrossing
desires—voices striving to drown one another
but ascending instead to unseen heights.

Moving on, unentangled, into the radiant darkness
I lose them, one by one. Stretches appear
as black ribbons. Hillsides heave
their heaps of nothing straight onto
the road, and dots of light are no longer

signals of fellow inhabitants, but the cold deaths
of distant stars.

Passing By

No bridge, just a newish
cul-de-sac where our sons
play, the cusp of manhood

spying them, forgetting us.
He drives by, waves: my anti-self
wearing my father's gaze

long into his future, my past.
We split long ago, this guy and I.
Yet I know where he's landed.

It rests in my bones. The thumbprint pharmacist
guiding his only way home. My alchemy
mixes with more uncertainty,

adds a dose of hope, and raises flames
from darker embers. I pick up my son
to the tune of disbelief

that I have come this far:
a ghost rider faking my way,
holding my life before me on a stick

and practicing a sorcery that writes surprises
in every prescription.

Beausoleil

Light does not meet the horizon
but enters the gray water
that ends in waves at my feet.

Small centuries huddle there
as Wordsworth rolls in, the silence
of Dostoyevsky, repetition of Stein.

Twenty years ago I was there—
on the other side of the mountain—
when the water was so clear you could fill

your cup, drink the blue sky,
and sleep through the ages
as fog found its way up to Dragon Lake

but never followed us. So now comes
Whitman, and Dickinson fading in,
melting like moonlight

too humble to see. My youth forms the rim
of Beausoleil Island; my words
have captured its waves. Together

we read them, watch them die,
then leave to write our own.

Poems That Got Away

They lie under field bones
next to highways that rose and fell
offering views I could not see.

They hang like ice crystals
where conversations occurred, brushing my shirt
as I ferry my way back to work.

Scattered among cooking debris in my kitchen,
flattened on the windowsills—I smell them
as I sleep in an unmade bed.

Words unravel at my back; stanzas
pop lynchpins suspended in the storm clouds
I flew through last week. Now I am

raising them, searching for their
remains among the ruins of a busy
life. Now they dig holes

through prisons of neglect,
reappearing in their finery, new colors
weaving a cloak for my shoulders,

a drawstring to hold in my palm.

Disappearing

Nearly twenty years
mean nothing next to this.
For what I remember is not

the sum of feats accomplished.
Nor do I count the gray hairs,
diverted eyes. I see a landscape

dressed in sadness—dark clothes
and a cool wind. A figure, my wife,
more alive than my salty dreams.

I hold more than her to my chest.
I hold all that I cannot hold.
So I wrap my arms tightly—

a quiet fit about her—
so someone may hear
the endless song in my head.

After all, what have we left
of a barren future
but the notes we paint

on a disappearing canvas—
the music of bitter, then sweet.

Fire Burned Through the Sacred Heart of Jesus

And left the yellow house
black and tan: bursts of shadow
at every window, cinder smell
and ever-evening for those
walking by. Anachronistic emptiness

now faces the pine-limned lake,
marring the settled suburb perfection
on either side. Jesus appears
on the screen door, his heart in flames
the only color left of this family's

kaleidoscopic past. His eyes
look out, his hands point inward,
and burnt yellow eats away
his hair. St. Margaret Mary Alacoque
once had a vision. She saw Jesus' heart

exposed and brilliant, as if
in flames, and interpreted this as a sign
that the world had turned away from him
and his all-consuming love. *We must
consecrate our homes to him,* she said,

till they burn by his example.

Gorky Park, 1986

There are rumors in the centers of trees
in Gorky Park.

The sounds coming from loudspeakers there
are absent.

The swans living in Gorky Park
are beautiful black, their beaks orange
and young gray.

A Ferris wheel spins circles
in the air, making winds
against the trees.

A man comes up to ask for a match,
not knowing what language to speak.

The young speak in corners.
The old do not speak.

The swans move within sight
of everyone.

There are playgrounds set up for amusement
and cafés closed for the evening.

It is seven o'clock.

No one is able to fill the quiet
as words grow heavy on trees.

Triptych

I.

Patchy clouds changing
all evening. The mountain
half-hidden, its color
undetermined.

Lake water
streaked, jagged edges
breaking dusk in two.

My box of soft pastels
lies unopened
as we move in from the chill
to sip dark wine.

II.

Curtains undrawn, light finds me
on the high bed at 2:30 AM:
an almost-half moon
poised in the crossed arms

of adjacent hills—a vantage point
we can only dream of
uncovered for an hour or two—

as it shines on black water
and animals freeze in their tracks.

III.

Re-awakened, I strain to raise
my head, this time met
by a horizontal band of tangerine
outdoing the sky. Hills

now silhouettes, I hear movement
in the battle of elements
that steams the lake, each white wisp

a character in the play of a dawn
I cannot keep up with
but may glimpse before the curtain falls.

A Tornado in the Garden

I look away, dismayed
at what wind will bring:
a potpourri of seasons

flying their cards of color. Every care
I had taken there disappears.
The result is unknown

and I must do the foretelling,
wondering whether gardening will endure
or go the way of literature and painting—

bright colors without direction,
things that are planted
without a seed.

Nature, Who Wants to Kill Me

Slipped a few bacteria into my lungs
and let them multiply there
as I lay shivering in the dark living room

looking through the window
at her stars and cloud-lit sky, lost
in her beauty.

Tuesday Cacophony

Crows caw in the morning
disguised as bravery
disguised as sorrow
disguised as wonder.

I wonder what pulls their parley
in so many directions,
what secrets are shared
when most of us are so busy
we can't distinguish utterance
from annoyance.

Could it be they refuse to pray,
and take the sun's cue for personal
gain—a cohort of chaos
to despise our race?

—or rather, a gathering
of black hearts encaged
in folklore and superstition

disguised as foolery
disguised as black holes,
as nicks of prescient time.

The Immensity of Being

A baseball flies high above
a city-lot field, spinning its yin/yang
of white and white. The players look up;
they too are caught in its slow motion,

uncertainty, complexity of being that entices
them all. Each has a new center of self—
thirty-five feet in mid-air, nothing
underneath, a changing perspective

of the immensity of themselves. The hills round out
and rivers cut a clearer course. Every city
and landscape they once disowned
comes back, to fill-in the scene

and prepare the way for this ball's
landing. The very air conducts time,
driving deeply into their refreshened lungs
like a chill, a brief removal

from the landed game, a twirling white madness
that must come to rest.

Birds May Outlive Us

Birds may outlive us.
Their needs are simple:
a tube of millet seeds,
violet evening light,
a crook in a backyard branch
in which to build a nest.

Sometimes I inspect my body:
wide shoulder blades in the mirror
where no wings grow. The pre-appointed
hands, unpredictable abdomen.

In my mouth, words. Seldom song.
I spend all day raking, pruning,
trying to keep out anything that wants in.

But oh, the sparrows
and scarlet tanagers resist.
They keep nimble to their form,
take note of their surroundings
then fall swiftly in the face
of beautiful unknowns.

Requesting Altitude

Above Cleveland I feel safe
sailing an ocean of air
inhabited by strange birds
of neither land nor sea—

They come from all directions,
glints of reddish silver streaming
through the clouds, requesting altitudes
from the surly voices below.

White currents obscure them
as the falling sun attests
to their anonymity, throwing us all
into a deeper sea of green.

It's no wonder we hold these patterns
while letting those collective voices
guide us, like conscience, through sky.

A Garden of Refuse

Don't give me flowers bordering the yard
in colors too pure to believe.

Don't give me sunlight unobstructed
by inclement weather, shining on grass

as green as the first living day.
Don't bring me overwhelming scents

nor the velvety petals of Earth's desire.
I'd rather sit in a moon-lit garden

of box springs and rusting cars,
a flattened pillow here and there,

abandoned electric stoves and smudgy dial
phones; maybe a lost earring (that tells

a story) and my grandfather's shoes.
I'd feel more akin to these things

and to those who made them. I'll laugh at the perfect
garden, curse it down, before those velvety petals

take me in, and Earth holds me silently
in the last laugh.

Fallen

The rose has fallen.
Snow drops white
as feathers, as windows.

It is a red candle,
not white: roselike.
Red as a Christmas
box. Advent has gone.

It is a wet snow,
Virginialike: holding
us together like
feathers in a box.

Snow curves into itself
like rose petals, filling
the earthbud: ground
soft as feathers.

A Humming Silence

Doing Push-ups

I have been doing push-ups
again, and I wonder what it is
I'm pushing up

or letting down. I can do a hundred
or two, or sit down and read
till I'm blue in the face.

Will I ever have enough energy
to say a prayer? The cat catching
dust motes seems to fare better.
He's only eaten a horsefly today,
and yet each mote compels him—

His hind legs lean like a kangaroo's;
my bobbing head won't bother him

as he paws the air, as if
he's seen mice, to lick
even two hundred motes.

The Year We Gave Up Coffee and Cigarettes

Everything seemed clear.
We had arrived at our roles
before the world turned to war.

We gave up simulating, too, bending
our traditions to meet this preconceived
arrival. Our minds cleared

along with our bodies. Little snow
fell, and summer brought endless
bounty. But then a fire cracked

and other alignments set themselves
too near: purity became folly
and folly dished herself up

as a familiar past. Now hair
grows long; life is a muddle.
Coffee warms our intentions

and we see only one thing at a time,
never the bitter end.

Tonight I Will Write a Beautiful Poem

Tonight I will write
a beautiful poem.

It will rest like a mourning dove
on a crooked branch without leaves.

It will be a mirror to my fine limbs
and startled face. My accomplishments

will find fault with its grandiose plan.
Street cats will stop and look up

as it passes by—a long shadow
owned by nothing.

A humming silence will transmit it
to bloodlines of other ages.

Reading in the Dark

His uniform was dark green
and black, his hair burnt
chestnut; a long black shadow
leading from his feet

out to the patterned floor.
(The piano player not yet come,
his keys ordered quietly
in black and white—waiting

for the wide room to fill
with unquiet, to catch their random
conversations, and turn them into song.)
But, for now, the worlds he reads

are set in grayed pages, their landscapes
lit by brilliant suns of the past.
The bartender tends his empty glasses;
their focused lenses stand ready

to blur long darknesses into light.

What Stirs the Creation

Heaven's gifts come not in boxes
but in spheres: they spin in union
and apart from one another,

bearing clotted matter within the void
of none. In this way all that intergalactic dust
is cleaned, condensed away

to leave space pure. Anything jagged, liquid,
or moving gravitates back to a ball
like the dough your grandmother rolled

for bread, picking up stray flakes and flecks
of flour. Rounded things feel better
in our hands, resting in their tender palms

like planets that have lost their way.
Even our bones must join with rounded edges,
our blood circulate, our memories work in reference

to arcs of time.

Here Where We Meet

Here where we meet
earth and sky
crab apple green

and emerald herald
stitching a ring
around the earth—

Here where we take
what is offered, leave
a trail of sorrows

but also evidence
spinning beyond control
a loud shout

our planet must bear
as she sheds her color
a volatile mantle

to make room
for those layers of artifact
she once dreamed

but could not call her own.

Instinct

I smell the past about me,
hanging in the trees, dug under
my garden. Body parts are
buried there. I see them
in my ancestors' eyes.

What one of us has done
will find us, one by one.

We carry the memory,
unleash its instinct
under government orders.

Listen: a raptor's call.
It bristles the blood—
gargled coo down the spine.

We've Been Told Nothing

We've been told nothing
of the sway of rye and barley
in Ukraine's occupied fields,

how they weigh with spirits
of the starved, overrun, shot.
We've been told nothing about the bloodroots

of American trees, the dark blue uniforms
moving against the holy night.
Or the way another body feels

after there is nothing left to feel,
its hearing gone, or sight—just a buzzing
too mechanical to be called human.

Meanwhile we've been basking
in our accomplishments, and making our children
walk the gangplank of getting More

without telling them how many
of them
have been left out, memories uninvited

to our tidy table. Only in twilight dreams
are we able to tell each other everything.
You awaken from the hurt

not knowing who's been told
and who must do the telling.

Plivitsa Lakes, Croatia

Greens falling from leaves;
blues from the sky; golds yellowing
the perimeter of hills; cloud reflections

showing us how still the water.
We walk the planked path
at lake's edge into the emerald

dream, the stark waterfall,
microclimes of moss and floating
flowers. We feel insulated

then gifted, dining on fresh
trout pulled from the view.
A woman sells pot cheese

seated, arm akimbo, staring off
to a future of gunfire
and holes that blast open

paradise. She is old enough to have known
other wars, but the one that is coming
is hidden to us: American tourists

too young to have seen what must
repeat, too happy in our seeded
expectations, loners in a world

where perception is fragile—
dreams wound in dreams
and others lost at the edges.

These Are the Boys We Send to War

The steamfitter sits cross-legged
on the stone floor, cracking his
hard-boiled breakfast egg.

He stretches to fit enclosures
for air, offering us a way
to stay alive: a loud banging mess

he works to precision. He nods hello
with eyes under a baseball cap,
lollipop in his mouth at 9 AM.

With no one to nurture him
he's lost his last childish weight,
unprepared to add the frame

of manhood. And yet he works
beyond his years, shaping our layer
of atmosphere, then walking away

from his gift: endless tracts
of life's quickening traces.

Colors

Having spent every Saturday morning of my childhood
studying the possibilities of the color wheel
and then their applications in the paintings

of the masters, I never liked many of the schemes I saw
in the clothes of Anglo-dominated
America—the red/white/blue or white/black,

orange/pink outdating navy/beige.
Something looked unfair, uncommitted
to the intricacies of emotion those stolid citizens

wore. For a brief period I found olive swirls,
terracotta tints, and burnished blues
collected in department store corners

permitted for experimental youth,
yet in final maturity we are all expected
to return to whatever dulls

the imagination, upholds the cold abstractions
we live by, making believe that men
should be as fair-faced as women,

trimmed as suburban shrubbery,
and as colorless in business
as ants pushing dirt uphill.

So imagine my surprise and terror
to find that we are bombing Afghans
who dress like magi and madonnas—

in colors we have worshipped on the walls
of the Uffizi, Hermitage, Louvre—
my wonder at where their colors come from;

whether they'll disappear, or find their way to the eyes
of other ten-year-olds a hemisphere away.

The European Spacecraft Lands on Mars
This Christmas Day

Boxes rip open; ribbons fly off
like falling shreds of a sunset
sky. Stars line windows

and eaves. As darkness rages
we force imaginations into
interiors. Rituals ring

in swanky color. Hands extend
to the most remote
acquaintances. Travelers clog

airways and ground. We drink
distillations of spirits, waiting
for light to return. And all this

slowly goes the way of dinosaurs
as science explains away
our most cherished traditions

but gives us one more mystery
that tells us not how to live
but sends us straight to the heart

of a wintry red desert—
ourselves.

One Year Later

(September 11, 2002)

On the way home,
sticks fallen everywhere. Branches
fallen, dangling from trees. A scatter

of living leaves, green, in patches
along the roads. Dust, dirt,
debris. A clear wind fed by a hurricane

parked far away. Wires
are down. Laundry, down.
All day we are remembering.

Bright sky, filled with wandering wind:
It came while we were away,
busy, planning our remembering.

Now our landscape is changed.
Buildings are down. Emotions
down. Our places of busyness

blown over the globe. This heavy, heart-felt
wind circling back to us, saying
"Nothing ever leaves this world."

"Sudan Was Not Allowed to Vote Because It Has Not Paid Its Dues"

As reported in The Times this day
in February, some change did not
change hands, black to white, and so

Sudan has no say on whether we will war
its distant Muslim cousins. Sudan,
whose land has been divided by oily leaders

and dusty land keepers, whose naked wrestlers
once sat strong on full shoulders,
whose starvation has sucked its purse

dry, whose prehistory gave these moneychangers
life, has not paid its dues.
It is not allowed to vote; cast out

from the human family—its progeny—
like a senile grandparent set to rot.
But the winds of ages carry drought

far and wide, and soon Sudan
will green over, its nakedness
will be once-again blessed

and those who once judged it will be lost
in blinding deserts.

This Is The End of the World

This is the end of the world:
a five-star resort in Phoenix,
a walk among gray rock, hares
and hummingbirds. The view—
its garden of popsicle palms

leading down to a city on edge.
I did nothing to earn this;
the ghosts of steel mills gather
at my back. In a minute they'll be gone.

Who wrote the rules of human tragedy?
One minute we're gasping for breath;
the next, summoning up blessings,
disregarding the rest. In the end
we become pointillist paintings in shifting

landscapes, colors that recombine
like facial expressions; or works
by Delacroix, layers of visions and schemes.
None of them quite finished.

To My Wife Flying Six Miles Above the Atlantic as I Fall Asleep in a Snowstorm

We drift into our separate pods
of silence: yours riding on air,
mine encased in muffled ice.

We sleep apart once again,
two winds hurling a violent atmosphere
to test our integrities. We hope for comfort

but find only artifice: this house,
your plane, layers of solace found only
in human ingenuity. Even our daybreaks

differ; we realize the night
has been forfeited, given not to sleep
but to our veneers of emptiness,

the planet unbearable as it spins
not to pull but to keep our breaths
apart. Your landing will set you

into a foreign cacophony, while I
will rise to meet the snow
and dismantle its silence

one shovelful at a time.

Fair Enough

Fair enough, we lie together
for the nth time, skin to skin,
a suspended animation of runaway

lives. We'd like to go back
to the place where life was nothing
but where it was: sparks flying

through a brilliant Irish air, burning up
our plans, interrupting idyllic views
for ourselves. Instead, we give in

to the long night, safe in our memories,
newly aligned to unpredictable purpose,
old mysteries. We awaken to distant piano notes

played by our son—Gershwin's Preludes—
and disregard considerations
of what comes next.

Acknowledgments

Caduceus: Colors, Fair Enough, I Love Your Tears, Polish Men, Pre-Adolescent Sons, Tuesday Cacophany

Connecticut Review: Last Words

CPR International: Doing Push-ups

Essential Love (anthology): Days of Love

Feile-Festa: Upon Rediscovering My Ancestors' Home in an Ancient Italian Town

Future Cycle Poetry: Driving Away from New York City

The Larcom Review: Lines

Louisiana Literature: My Mother Straightens Her Babushka

The MacGuffin: Maria Antonia Waits for Her Twin

Palimpsest: Dismembering the Swing Set, Sam

Paper Street: A Pittsburgh Christmas

Poetry for Peace (anthology): These Are the Boys We Send to War

Poetry Repair: Gorky Park, 1986

Voices in Italian Americana: What Stirs the Creation